SCARFE Land

OPPOSITE: THE AUTHOR IN FULL HUNTING KIT

GERALD SCARFE

SCARFE Land

THE LOST WORLD

HAMISH HAMILTON · LONDON

DESIGNED BY CRAIG DODD

Published by the Penguin Group
27 Wrights Lane, London W8 5TZ, England
Viking Penguin Inc, 40 West 23rd Street, New York, New York 10010, U.S.A.
Penguin Books Australia Ltd, Ringwood, Victoria, Australia
Penguin Books Canada Ltd, 2801 John Street, Markham, Ontario, Canada L3R 1B4
Penguin Books (N.Z.) Ltd, 182-190 Wairau Road, Auckland 10, New Zealand

Penguin Books Ltd, Registered Offices: Harmondsworth, Middlesex, England

First published in Great Britain 1989 by
Hamish Hamilton Ltd

Copyright © 1989 by Gerald Scarfe

1 3 5 7 9 10 8 6 4 2

British Library Cataloguing in Publication Data
CIP data for this book is available from the British Library

ISBN 0-241-12859-5

Typeset by Keymark Graphics, London
Colour separations by Bright Arts, Hong Kong
Printed in Italy by Printers Srl, Trento
Bound by L.E.G.O., Vicenza

For Katie

THE LOST WORLD: PROLOGUE

 I could feel their eyes on me, watching, waiting, in the inky darkness. I trod carefully on the soft grass – there could be traps ahead. The creatures were near: I could smell them, and occasionally a small sound – an escape of breath or a low grunt – would betray their presence. From time to time the full pale green moon would break from behind a scudding cloud, picking out a glistening eye before it disappeared into the lush, dense foliage.

§ I had come to this strange land out of curiosity, in the spirit of the great animal artist Audubon, not with a gun but with a pen, to capture its beasts on paper.

§ I had been excited by tales of exotic creatures and mythical monsters: the sexy Uniporn, the frightening Tebbitsaurus, the great White Bird of Pray in the Sky and the beasts across the mountains – the Bush Eagle, the Sweet and Sour Peking Dragon, and the Perestroika.

§ I cannot say exactly where this world is, only that it is nearer than we think.

§ There was a shiver in the air, and the early morning sun threw long shadows across the wet grass as I started the climb to the plateau in search of my quarry. I was travelling light, carrying only my drawing materials, a small tent, change of clothing and provisions.

§ Below me an entertaining flock of harmless dahlings *(Thespian Dearboyus)* sat in a circle (some in the stalls). 'Dahling you were wonderful!!' they chirrupped, looking at themselves in their dressing room mirrors. 'Was I all right, dahling?' 'Super, dahling, loved it, dahling!'

§ The Watch Bird *(Rhesus Moggus)*, with his long neck, eyed me disapprovingly from where he stood silently waiting for sex and violence before nine o'clock.

§ Capture wasn't always easy; sometimes I would circle my prey for hours with intense concentration, trying to pin him down with my pen, stabbing at him from time to time. Just when I thought I had him he would disappear into thin air, leaving only wisps of smoke.

§ Although I searched and searched I could not find the Lesser Spotted Rushdie (*Salman en Croute*).

§ On the second day my journey took me through the dust storms of the wastelands, with their cracked grey concrete runways and contaminated hedgerows festooned with tiny shreds of dirty torn plastic, and across fields laced with poison.

§ The stones felt sharp underfoot and pressed through my shoes as, with great care, I descended the crumbling, eroded cliffs to the ever rising sea. Down there by the polluted shore the waves broke yellow with industrial waste, the bodies of ruined birds, poisoned fish and bloated seals rolled and ebbed in the oily sludge. A light breeze sprang up, catching tiny scraps of shredded plastic and swirling them into a miniature tornado.

§ On the third day the earth shook. Black smoke hung in a blood red sky above a bubbling crater. The lip of the volcano was encrusted black, seething with greedy writhing bodies lured by the molten gold which spilled white hot from the crater, burning many to death. It was a fascinating, if horrific, sight. They crashed and sprawled over one another, jaws dripping, gouging eyes and devouring each other in an effort to reach the glowing gold.

§ Through the grey-blue mists, from across the scarred and pitted landscape, I heard the distant screams of those poor creatures: the victims of brutes like the Noriega who feed on the strife and misery of their fellows.

THE NORIEGA *(Cocainus Crack Pot)*

§ Long ago I had heard of the mystical Labyrinth, home of the MinorTories and Labourytes, where the decisions that sway lives are written in stone by incompetents. I had read strange tales of the wicked Ptorydactyl, whose graven image in the shape of two lions flanked the Labyrinth.

§ Legend had it that the Ptorydactyl had built her eyrie high in the mountains, so at six-thirty one morning I shouldered my pack and set off to find her. During that day it rained; great thunder clouds hung in the leaden sky.

§ After an exhausting day's climb I neared the summit, made camp on a perilously narrow ledge and settled down for the night. I fell into an uncomfortable sleep. When I awoke at five-thirty the next morning it was bitterly cold: with fumbling fingers I opened my sketch pad and prepared to wait . . .

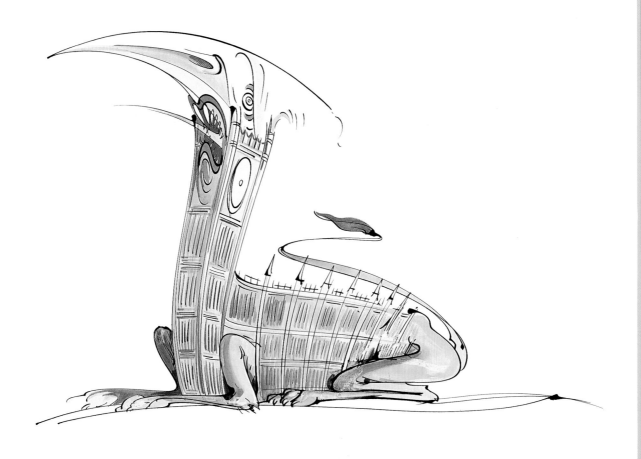

§As the morning light from the slate-grey sky spilled across the barren Downing mountains the Ptorydactyl busied herself about her eyrie. There was so much to do. She tidied her hair and sharpened her razor bill. She must make herself look nice – sympathetic, no, caring was the word today. She wanted to create a caring image when she opened her first DIY hospital. A brilliant idea, a DIY hospital, no staff, just do it yourself medical equipment. You chose your op, picked up the necessary equipment, paid at the automatic cheque-out and simply did your own operation. It would give old and sick creatures with a defeatist point of view a new incentive, give them some get up and go.

§As I watched from a safe distance she launched herself from her icy ledge and her leathery wingtips scraped the hard crust of snow in the Westland valley. There were those who said that her gimlet eyes were blind to suffering but what, indeed, about the time she cried the crystal tear for her father, that split the earth asunder when it fell – maybe she could do that again. She would try. She had a Capodimonte model of the dear creatures who fought for her in the Falklands which sometimes brought a lump to her throat.

 THE SABRE-TOOTHED PTORYDACTYL *(Thatcherlottus)*
Habitat: Late Miocene period, Finchley.
Cry: Not one of us.
REMARKS: PredaTory beast. Nasty habit of rolling on and eating the weaker of its young. Member of the conservative species. Suddenly turns green if it suits her. Note the formidable dentition.

PLATE *1*

§I picked up my sketch pad and followed as the Ptorydactyl, carried on the fierce winds of monetarism, sped over the great North-South divide in the direction of the Labyrinth, where her baying Minortories obediently waited. She amused herself by diving briefly to scatter a clutch of Pinter hedgehogs. She had crushed the union dinosaurs and squashed the Galtieri slug (Gotcha!), what was a mere hedgehog? Definitely not 'one of us', dear. Her mocking laugh echoed across the dead valley, 'Frit Frit!' she shrieked. 'Frit Frit!' At the Labyrinth the dead Howe sheep and a hurd of Douglasses skulked nervously.

§ The Cold Curried Chicken strutted out to meet the Ptorydactyl. She was an ambitious, pushy bird, with a voice as shrill as a suburban car alarm, but she had a calm inner strength, a secret of her own: she knew she was always right, a great source of strength in trying times and, although she had been completely plucked several times (they'd even complained about her smelly eggs), she had always been proved right in the long run.

 THE COLD CURRIED CHICKEN *(Salmonella Vindaloo)*
Habitat: The Labyrinth.
Cry: Wrap up.
REMARKS: Rising in pecking order again. Foot in mouth disease. Hen bird, but also talks cock.

PLATE 2

§ I soon tired of those frightful creatures and moved on. I walked all day in the hot sun when I came upon a sleek pink porker who sat contentedly in the corner of his sty scoffing copious amounts of money. He appeared to be asleep but, suddenly and with frightening ferocity, he inflated and then, with slow deliberation, swelled to an enormous size until he began slowly to leave the ground and float away over the tree-tops.

 THE PIGGY BANK *(Awesome Lawson Porkus)*
Habitat: Next door to the Ptorydactyl.
Cry: I'm on course, it's only a blip.
REMARKS: He'll burst if he gets much rasher.

PLATE 3

§As dusk fell I made my way back to the dark silhouette of the Labyrinth outlined against the blood-red sky. The gargantuan coarse-hided Tebbitsorearse stood in the doorway, his tail switching mechanically. A Heffer, returning late from a Union meeting, had the misfortune to cross the Tebbitsorearse's path. As I watched terrified, the huge monster bent forward with surprising swiftness and with his yellow poisonous teeth bit off the Heffer's head, "On yer bike!" he snarled. "On yer bike!" I ran for my life.

 THE TEBBITSOREARSE *(Normanis Gargantua)*
Habitat: Paloecene period.
Cry: On yer bike!
REMARKS: A horrific sight, full twenty feet tall and fifty feet long. A powerful body carried on strong hind legs. The fore limbs are small and stunted in growth.

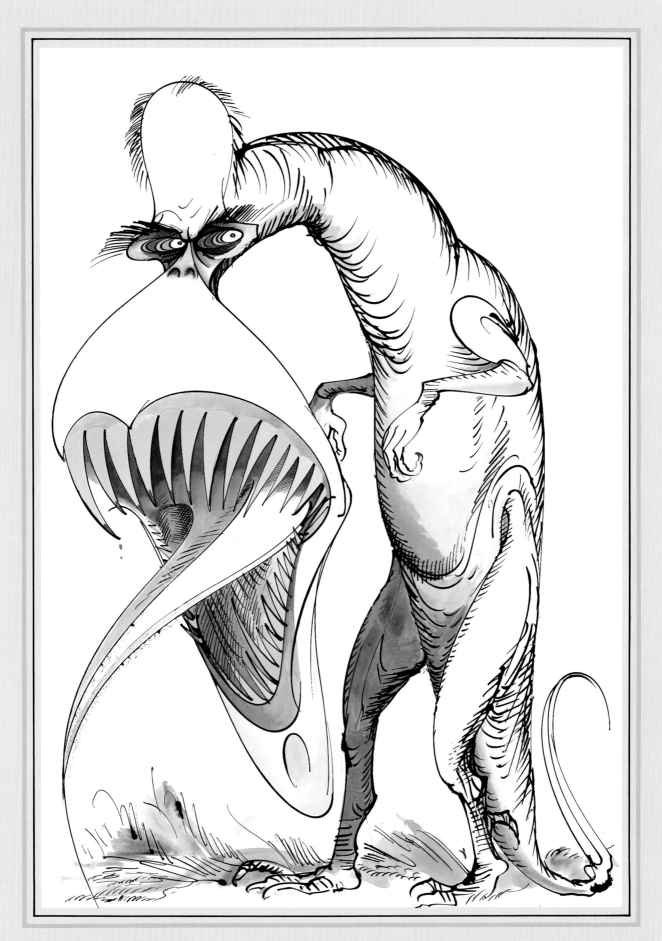

PLATE 4

§*I must have fallen asleep for when I awoke the sun was high and so was the Pizzdazza Newt who reeled across the green fairways towards me shouting "Fore!" and "This way to the clubhouse".*

§*He bounced off a rock, spun round and croaked in a startled voice, "Cripes, I thought that was the old bat. Where is she?" he said, looking over his shoulder shakily.*

"She's in the Ptorydactyl's eyrie," I replied.

"What, old boy?"

"The Ptorydactyl's eyrie."

"You're damn right she is," he said as he fell into a bunker.

 THE PIZZDAZZA NEWT *(Denis Propupbarus)*
Habitat: The Clubhouse.
Cry: Mine's a large one!
REMARKS: Mate of the Ptorydactyl, sometimes seen in tow, surrounded by caddie flies.

PLATE 5

§I walked away through the tall grasses and made my way down to the swollen oily sea. There, marooned on the detergent-flecked shore, the beached White Whale moaned and groaned about that bloody old bat. She had bitten him half to death in the guise of the Great White Shark years ago, and he had never recovered. All he had left now was his organ, and that wasn't all it had been. He occasionally played it, but is seemed out of tune, and she never listened. 'Hear today and deaf tomorrow, that's her trouble,' he blubbered. 'KEEP UP AT THE BACK THERE!' bellowed the Ptorydactyl.

 THE BEACHED WHITE WHALE *(Heath Blubberatus)*
Habitat: Europe.
Cry: Occasionally.
REMARKS: Humpback whale, so called because he has the hump. Harpooned by the miner birds and has never really recovered.

PLATE 6

§ Down in the Westland arboretum I heard the low growls of the despicable Heselswine as he lay in wait for the Ptorydactyl, biding his time to rip her throat open.

 THE HESLESWINE *(Ambitious Bastardus)*
Habitat: The outskirts of Westland.
Cry: Aren't I gorgeous.
REMARKS: Waiting for the main chance.

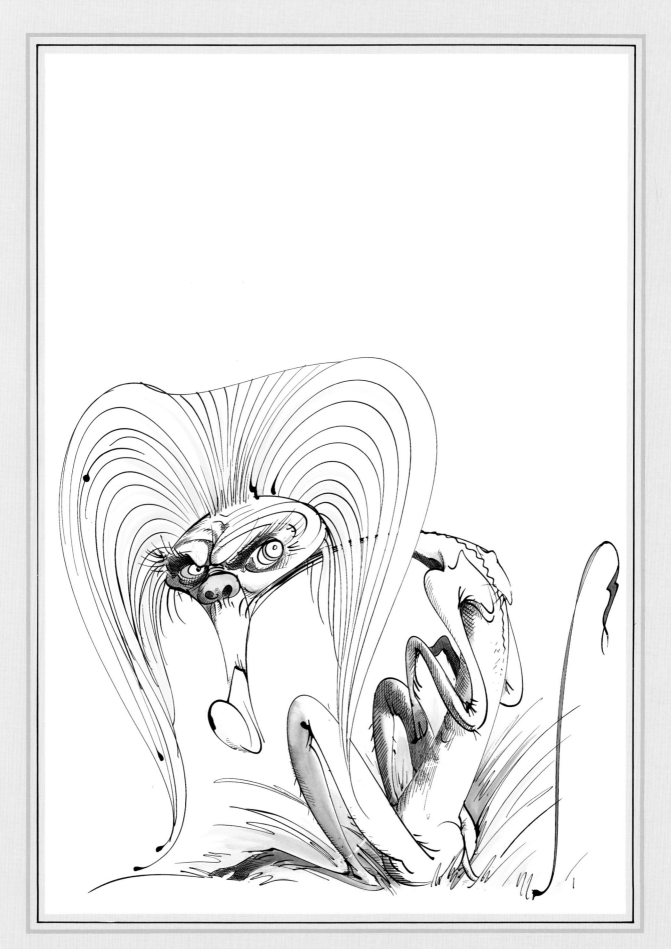

PLATE 7

§Down in the dark dankling wood, wet black clanging in the valleys, the old Welsh dragon lay in his lair repeating favourite phrases and murmuring sweet nothings to himself. His fire was out but still small puffs of hot air leaked from every orifice. He had done well, he told himself. He had acquitted himself well last Thursday, or was it Wednesday? How they had all laughed when he had risen to his feet in the Labyrinth and – ha ha ha! – oh boy, it made him laugh even now when he thought of it! – he said – no, don't laugh – well a rather clever thing really . . . he said to the Ptorydactyl, he'd said . . . "Up yours, you immaculate misconception!" Ha ha ha! . . . Really remarkably clever, now he thought of it. "Good on you, Boyo!" he heard himself saying. The old Welsh wizardry was working again. Wit was not dead. Aneurin would have loved it, literally loved it, Boy. With a sigh he fell asleep, contentedly. I tiptoed away, not wishing to disturb him.

 THE LESSER WELSH SPECKLED DRAGON (*Kinnockus Pillockus Rhetoric Farticus*)
Habitat: The Valleys of Politics.
Cry: I promise I will only use the bomb for winning votes.
REMARKS: Lurks in the shadows making sudden impetuous forays into the limelight to crack a joke or slip over, and then disappears again. Nominal wings, incapable of flight.

PLATE 8

§ The mad Hattersley hare had just finished a lovely lunch, and jolly good it was too, spoilt only by that silly chap asking him about the defence policy yet again.

 THE MAD HATTERSLEY HARE *(Lièvre en Gélee)*
Habitat: On the other side of de-fence.
Cry: We're on our way.
REMARKS: Hare today and gone tomorrow.

PLATE 9

§The Dodo came bouncing down the Socialist hill, carrying his looking glass. He didn't seem to know he was dead. He stopped to admire himself. "Is there anybody who wants to know anything?" he said to some disinterested sparrows. "Look out, it's Owen," muttered one. "Anything at all about any subject – just ask me." The sparrows turned away and examined the grass. The Dodo stood, puzzled by the silence, and then disappeared behind a bush. Moments later he reappeared in a bright yellow set of feathers. "Good afternoon! I'm from the B.O.D.F.– The bird of a different feather party," he explained, preening his new plumage. The sparrows moved away, giving little dry coughs of embarrassment.

 THE DEADASA DODO *(S.D.P. Superior Davidus Party)*
Habitat: Nowhere really.
Cry: I'm too young and beautiful to die.
REMARKS: All the dodos I know are stuffed.

PLATE *10*

§I approached with extreme caution as the Queen of the beasts lay in her den idly eating corgis dipped in honey and gazing across her crown estates. It was a wonderful day. Her husband the Great Auk-ward Busturd Edinbird was killing some animals down on the estate, she could hear their squeals. I felt out of place so, bowing low, I made my exit.

 THE ROYAL LION *(Reign Hanoverus)*
Habitat: Buckingham Palace, Windsor Castle, Sandringham and the Royal yacht *Britannia.*
Cry: My bustard and I . . .
REMARKS: Much-liked Royal beast, appears on Christmas Day just after the pudding. Fears no one except the Ptorydactyl.

PLATE *11*

§ *"Bugger!" an irritable foreign-looking bird stuck his head out of the Royal bunker. "You have incurred the Royal displeasure," he cried. "Don't think you'll get a bloody knighthood, or I'm not Greek! – Out of my way," he bellowed, pushing past. "You're buggering up the environment."*

 THE GREAT AUKWARD BUSTURD *(Crested Edinbird)*
Habitat: His mate's lair.
Cry: Bloody Hell!
REMARKS: Irritable, foul-mouthed creature who preserves other species by hunting and killing them. Opinionated, unsympathetic, intolerant and tetchy.

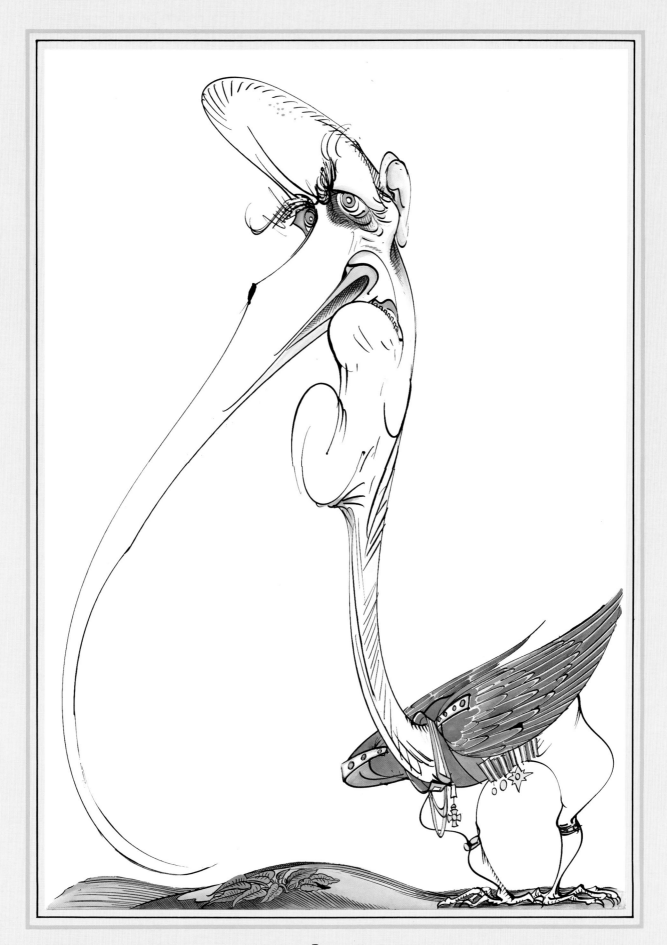

PLATE *12*

§ *The Right Royal Charlie sat on top of a concrete, steel and glass carbuncle surveying his future kingdom and wept. "It's ghastly!" he wailed. "Absolutely ghastly!" Lead fumes drifted past and stained his hunting pink and before him mile upon mile of ugly termite hills stretched as far as the eye could see (which wasn't very far).*

§ *"It's ghastly!" he choked. "The fruit is poisoned, the meat is poisoned, the water is poisoned, the very air itself is poisoned . . . Oh, woe is me! I am born to be king of a ruined land."*

§ *"Privatise it!" said the passing Ptorydactyl. "That's the solution. Privatise it."*

THE RIGHT ROYAL CHARLIE *(Heir Recedus)*
Habitat: The mountain top.
Cry: Absolutely ghastly!
REMARKS: A royal and gentle beast, constantly disturbed by his environment. Wanders off-piste, worrying about the ozone layer and seeking the succour of fragrant blooms amongst the carbuncles.

PLATE *13*

§There are some parts of the land that the creatures have not spoilt – but not many. It was a glorious morning as I strolled through the summer meadows around Old Fields. Up there in the Haute Couture the air is heavy with the scent of Chanel No. 5 and the trees are hung with Crêpe de Chine and Heavy Tulle. I felt light of heart and my joy was unbounded when I caught sight of the beautiful and elegant Clothes Horse. She cantered into view surrounded by a cloud of swirling multi-coloured social butterflies and gossip flies, dancing and eddying in the breeze. She paused and stood admiring herself, this rare creature, in a diamond and sapphire pool. And then suddenly, just like that, she changed all her clothes.

 THE CLOTHES HORSE *(Dianus Principia)*
Habitat: Fashion houses.
Cry: Okay Ya!
REMARKS: Much photographed creature.

PLATE *14*

§A huge freckled moon-face stuck a large chin over a vast yellow hill covered with purple spots. "Wacko!" it said. "Time for another jolly old holiday, what? Now where did I put my baby, oh yah, nurse has got it. Right off we go. Have you seen Andy?" Suddenly the vast yellow hill moved! – it was Fergie. "Where is he? I'm going to bloody well sit on him if he goes off like this again." I shuddered at the thought – and moved quickly on.

 THE GIGANTIC FERGIE *(Yorkus Elephantiatus)*
Habitat: Snowy slopes.
Cry: Wacko, I've caught a good 'un here.
REMARKS: An enthusiastic creature of the galumptious Sloane species. Method of kill – sitting on and smothering adversary with enormous ugly frocks.

PLATE 15

§ A good night's sleep and I rose at six thirty sharp.
A fine frosty morning as I made my way over the dew-soaked grass. My thoughts were interrupted by a piercing "Tally Ho!" The sturdy frame and fine fetlocks of the Royal Filly sailed over the hedge and landed with a resounding thwack amongst a swarm of gossip flies, quietly feeding on some rock creatures' droppings. They were up and buzzing about her withers before she could say "Naff orf!"

 THE ROYAL FILLY *(Centaur Autocraticus)*
Habitat: Gatcombe Park.
Cry: Naff orf!
REMARKS: Half-woman half-horse. Strong-willed creature with a fine temper. Good in the rough. Three-day eventer. Ten hands. Six to four on. Tote.

PLATE *16*

§The Silly Ass leapt over a five-barred gate, grinned and then jumped over another five-barred gate. It was a way of life. It was something to do.

 THE SILLY ASS *(Marcus Foggus)*
Habitat: Badminton.
Cry: Er . . . er . . . er . . .
REMARKS: Not a good runner, form middling to bad, used to cover the Royal Filly.

PLATE *17*

§It was a lovely morning in St James's and the Old Duck sailed by merrily bobbing up and down on gin and tonic.

 THE OLD DUCK *(Queen Mummus)*
Habitat: Clarence Lake.
Cry: Mine's a large one.
REMARKS: Much loved old duck, waves a lot.

PLATE *18*

§ I dived into the murky waters of the Legal Sea. The old Lobster sat in his crevice at the bottom, his feelers explored the current that ran past his home and served to warn the small fry, the tiddlers and molluscs, that he was someone of note. On his head he wore a wig made of seaweed tied with pink ribbon. He looked bored. A well-oiled silken barracuda danced before him. "You see, my Lord," he carped, "you cannot allow it. They should have no right of audience. Potted shrimps cannot speak to you, they must speak to me and I will speak to you then you will speak to me and I will speak to them. They must keep their plaice."

§ The Lobster, who up until then had been quite reasonable, turned bright red with rage.

§ I could hold my breath no longer and rose to the surface in a cloud of bubbles.

 LOBSTER MACKAY *(Homardus Chancelloris Legalis)*
Habitat: The Law Courts.
Cry: Silence!
REMARKS: A large crustacean, related to shrimps. Large legal clause, used for defence.

PLATE *19*

§ Runcie, the Church Cat, lay curled in the warm sunlight that streamed through the great mullioned window. He had a lot to muse about as he sat on his window ledge and let forth a constant stream on this and that and the way things are and were and would be etcetera, but no-one listened, not even his runcible wife who lay on the piano dead-heading flowers in an old vase.

 RUNCIE, THE CHURCH CAT *(Feline Canterburius)*
Habitat: A window ledge on Lambeth Palace.
Cry: Women's ordination, homosexual priests, world in peril, etc., etc.
REMARKS: Read all about it!

PLATE *20*

§*I sat sketching under a hot afternoon sky when the rustle of dry silken wings disturbed my thoughts. The Great White Bird of Pray in the Sky swooped low over the Vatican Mountains and his huge blue-grey shadow flickered across the expectant trusting faces upturned below. They knew by his smoke that he had returned. He came by what they call the rhythm method at a certain time of the month. "What shall we do?" they cried. "We are lost." The Great White Bird of Pray wheeled in the sky. "Thou shalt not pill," he said from a great height.*

 THE GREAT WHITE BIRD OF PRAY IN THE SKY *(Popemobilus Vaticanus)*
Habitat: Vatican mountains.
Cry: In domino patri.
REMARKS: Leaves a trail of incense.

PLATE *21*

§ *"ME! ME!" sang the Fettucine Nightingale. "ME! ME!"*

 THE FETTUCINE NIGHTINGALE *(Pavarotti Giganticus)*
Habitat: Italy.
Cry: Ah per l'ultima volta.
REMARKS: Glorious song, eats spaghetti vongole, fettucine pomadoro, gnocchi con formaggio and tagliatelle bolognese.

PLATE 22

§It was late evening when I reached the spangled rocks in search of the glittering Rock creatures. Jackson's Chameleon (Michaelis Plasticus) *lay sprawled on the green astro turf, loud music playing in the background. Suddenly he jerked to his feet in the most peculiar way and began to walk backwards, each of his limbs moving independently. Then the most amazing thing happened: slowly his nose got smaller, his lips grew slimmer and – most extraordinary of all – his skin grew lighter. I couldn't believe it. Before my very eyes this chameleon had turned into another creature – that Supreme bird of Paradise* Dianus Rossos. *Astounding.*

 JACKSON'S CHAMELEON *(Michaelis Plasticus) (Dianus Rossos)*
Habitat: An oxygen tent.
Song: I'm bad/Ain't no mountain high enough.
REMARKS: Rock creatures entertain other animals, receiving huge amounts of adulation and cash, which sends them stark staring mad.

PLATE 23

§ In the shadows of the night in the middle of a clearing sat the Tyger, sobbing his heart out. 'She caught me with a left and then she caught me with a right, and then KO'd me with a million dollars', he cried.

§ Then he got up and ran into a tree.

 THE TYGER *(Tyson Wallopus)*
Habitat: The ring.
Cry: Seconds out!
REMARKS: Champion heavyweight of the world.

PLATE 24

§ *The next morning I strolled in brilliant warm sunshine along the spray-drenched shore of the Cape. With horror I saw the dorsal fin of the Spielbird's wife (his most expensive production) bearing down on him through the rich seas. "What's Jaws is mine!" she cried.*

THE SPIELBIRD III *(Milliondollar Grossus)*
Habitat: A set in the rushes of the Holly woods.
Cry: Phone lawyer.
REMARKS: Close encounters of the marital kind.

PLATE 25

§*Up at Sunset; a warm but foggy day. I climbed up through the exotic Gucci plants and tall Maserati palms of the Holly Woods and found myself in Laurel Canyon. I was in search of a novel and alluring creature. Following her heady scent I made my way with difficulty through the dank-smelling undergrowth and strange-looking fungi. All at once, as if by magic, the fog cleared and I caught my first glimpse of the magnificent Uniporn. She stood revealed in all her glory on a heap of steaming novels, a permanent horn right through the middle of her mind. I could see every detail of her throbbing body, heaving breasts, erect nipples, damp flanks and firm, taut, rounded buttocks – no wonder wombats went crazy. I decided to approach her:*

'Good morning' I said.

She turned towards me, breasts heaving, nipples erect, etc., etc. 'Are you talking to moi, ------? You're full of ----! Get the ---- out of here!!'

§*This left me, pen in hand, feeling disappointed, and that there was . . . I don't know . . . something slightly vulgar about her. I decided to make my escape before she cast her spell on me.*

 THE UNIPORN *(Coitus Jackie Uninterruptus Collins)*
Habitat: Beverly Hills.
Cry: Bonk! Bonk!   Bonk! Bonk!
REMARKS: Obsessed with, and always examining, her own and others' sexual organs.

PLATE 26

§The Old Prairie Gipper wandered absentmindedly through the white mists of time across the parched floor of the valley quietly humming "A Four-Legged Friend" to himself. While I sketched he sat sadly for a moment amongst the whitening bones of the Republican elephant's graveyard asking himself over and over again: Who am I? Was I implicated? Who ordered the veal cutlet? A cold wind blew from North and he shivered. He waved a small flag in his trunk to cheer himself up and dreamt of the Great Days, the Great Fights and the Great Muddles, until Nancy came to fetch him. "Come on, Bonzo – bedtime." Slowly he rose to his feet and disappeared into the mist, leaving only a small indentation in the shifting white sand.

 THE OLD PRAIRIE GIPPER *(Pacadom Reaganmortis)*
Habitat: Disneyland.
Cry: Where am I?
REMARKS: Frequent periods of hibernation, or naps. Out to grass.

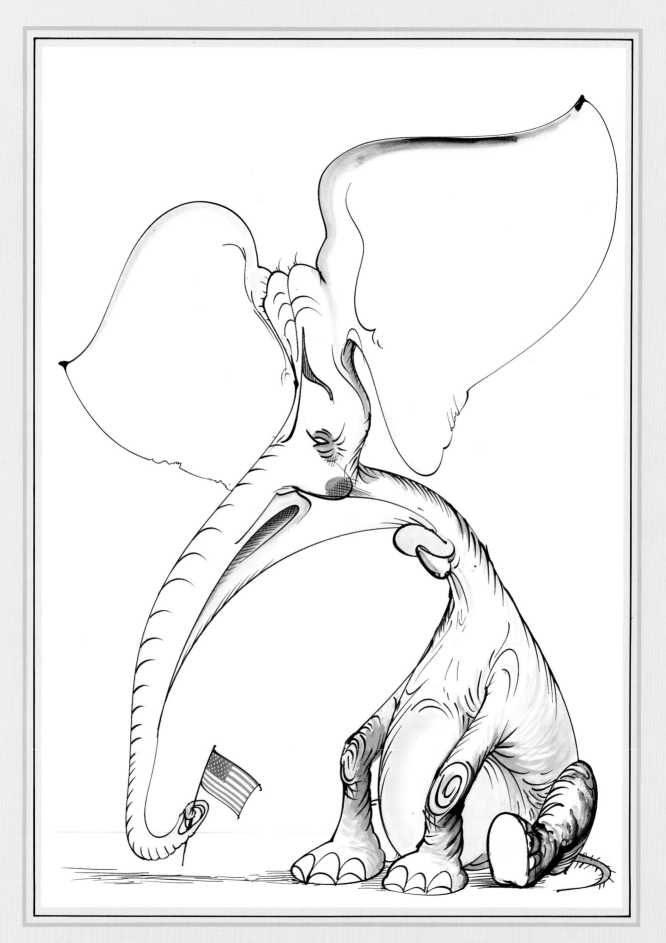

PLATE 27

§I was strolling along the Potomac, marvelling at the brilliant oranges and golds of the Fall, when there was a rustling and crackling amongst the Bushes that fringed the White House lawn and the Eagle appeared blinking in the bright light – "Oh, hi!" he croaked hesitantly. "Er, . . . have a nice day." There was more movement and a loud crackling sound and the Quayle fell out of a tree spreadeagling him on the ground. "Oops," grinned the Quayle. "Just trying to avoid the draft." The old eagle looked embarrassed and dusted down his dry old feathers with care. He seemed depressed and stood gazing at the ground for a while. "I sure can, er . . . pick them," he muttered. "The world sure is a big place," beamed the Quayle, walking into a cowpat.

 THE BUSH EAGLE *(Presidentus Godhelpus)*
Habitat: The Oval Office.
Song: I'm bushed.
REMARKS: Fairly new to the job, but already quite disarming.

PLATE 28

§*'Wow!' said the Quayle, 'only a heartbeat away!'*

 THE GOBBLEDEGOOK QUAYLE *(Dismalis Dimmus)*
Habitat: Only a heartbeat away!
Cry: Only a heartbeat away!!
REMARKS: Only a heartbeat away!!!

PLATE 29

§ I sat huddled in the bleak snowy wastes, my frost-bitten fingers refusing to grip the pencil. After his long hibernation in the cruel and frozen Stalin mountains, the Perestroika emerged blinking from his chrysalis into the cold blue morning light. There had been many, many, long, long winters but now a warm pink glow spread across the grey ice. It was beginning to thaw, cracks had appeared. Could it really be spring at last?

 THE PERESTROIKA *(Lepidoptera Kremlinis)*
Habitat: Kremlin.
Cry: Glasnost.
REMARKS: Remarkable if true.

PLATE 30

§On the far side of the world the sweet and sour Peking dragon slowly and deliberately unfurled and stretched himself. He had shed most of his old dull Grey Mao skin except around the head and by now had grown to two billion hands in length – an awesome sight. I watched the scaly new young body rising up in agony, twisting and writhing. It was revolting. I had the feeling it would tear off its feudal head, but, to my horror, the head reared violently and ripped the young flesh apart.

 THE SWEET AND SOUR PEKING DRAGON *(Deng Xiaoping)*
Habitat: China.
Cry: Long live democracy.
REMARKS: Number 1997 on the Chinese menu is a Hong Kong take-away.

PLATE *31*

§ *I followed the long, glistening trail down the Rue de Socialism and over the Place de la Bastille before I found l'Escargot. There he sat mournfully reciting Rimbaud on top of a glass pyramid.*

 L'ESCARGOT *(Gastropod Mitterrand)*
Habitat: Palais de l'Elysee.
Cry: Le changement!
REMARKS: Best with garlic.

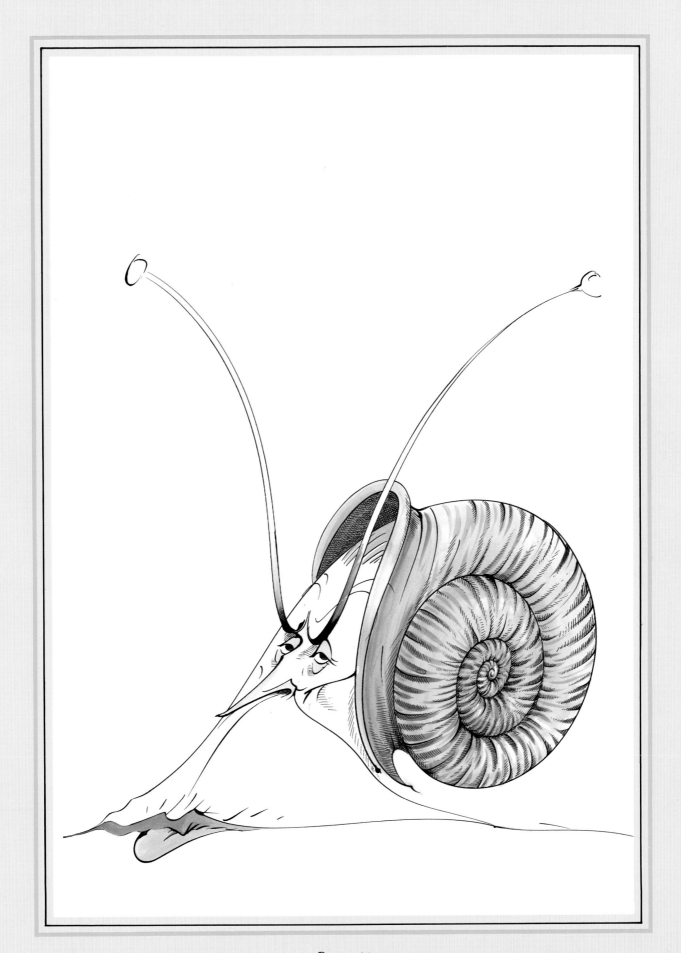

PLATE *32*

§Through the desert air the Ghaddfly zinged and zapped, switching this way and that, his brilliant colours warning of his dangerous bite. Diving, he suddenly hovered and immediately went into fast reverse. He dived into his tent. They would soon feel his sting.

 THE GHADDFLY *(Odonata Libya)*
Habitat: The desert.
REMARKS: Silently folds his tent and steals away.

PLATE 33

§I sat cross-legged, engrossed in my work, deep in the ridged sand dunes. The arid air dried my watercolours the moment they touched the cartridge paper. A long, purple shadow fell across my painting and I raised my eyes to see, over the shimmering desert in the scorching heat, an unshaven, extended camel padding through the nomadic wastes of undulating sand on his seemingly never-ending quest for an oasis. Ever since he could remember he had been homeless. I watched as he became a tiny speck on the liquid horizon and disappeared as though he had been a mirage.

 THE ARAFAT CAMEL *(Camelas Yasser)*
Habitat: Nowhere.
Cry: Al Fatah.
REMARKS: Can travel indefinitely as he stores a large arsenal in his hump.

PLATE 34

§ A leathery creature with eyes like silver bullets and tiny needle-sharp teeth darted across the road in a cloud of dry red dust, up a Palestinian camel's trouser leg, and bit him in the Gaza Strip.

 THE SHAMIR *(Premierus Israeli)*
Habitat: The Knesset.
Cry: It is written, it is mine!
REMARKS: Very territorial.

PLATE 35

§ It was a beautiful morning. Rajiv the flying jumbo banked steeply in the clear blue Indian skies and prepared for touch-down. Below, tragedy waited, and they would take away his wings and make him head of state.

 RAJIV GANESH *(Gandhi Indianus)*
Habitat: Congress party.
Cry: I'm still Mr Clean.
REMARKS: Seen here trying to take off.

PLATE 36

§ *Rattle, rattle . . . the slimy snake slipped and slithered, slid and slunk over the Manhattan rocks. His hard bright eye fell upon a hoard of glittering loot. He was a greedy little devil. Whenever he saw something he wanted he swallowed it up – just like that. You wouldn't believe how much he'd swallowed, and as he moved it rattled inside him. The more he swallowed – rattle, rattle – the less he moved – rattle, rattle – and the less he moved the more he swallowed, until one day he stopped.*

 THE RATTLESNAKE *(Thieving Marcos)*
Habitat: In exile.
Cry: Absolute cobras! We are innocent.
REMARKS: Female of the species tends to hoard hundreds of pairs of shoes.

PLATE *37*

§ *"I'm such a wicked wicked bird,"* sobbed the Bob Hawke. *"I've led such a wicked life,"* he blubbed, *cocking one eye to see what effect he was having. Some nearby Dundee crocodiles were in tears too but those who were more fly said, "He's up to something! What's he trying to cover up this time, the old bastard?"*

 THE BOB HAWKE *(Accipiter Australianus)*
Habitat: Down under.
Cry: Frequently.
REMARKS Quick, dashing flier, with broad wings and back. A long tail gives it the ability to fly deftly through frequent oncoming missiles.

PLATE 38

§I made my way along a dry river bed. The sun by this time being very hot, I stopped for some refreshment. A distant bellowing came to my ears and I dropped on all fours and crawled along the river bed until I could peer around the next bend. The Hippopotomax lay wallowing in the mud, surrounded by drunken bad gnus. "More, more, more, MORE!" he cried. His gigantic jaws dripped with sheer greed. "MORE POWER! MORE TO SPOIL!!" From time to time he admired himself in his cracked Mirror.

§I only had time to make a quick sketch before he spotted me. I made an excuse and left.

 THE HIPPOPOTOMAX *(Maxwellus Pergamon)*
Habitat: Liechtenstein.
Cry: Rule Britannia.
REMARKS: Enormous bullying thick-skinned creature. Eats trees. Swallows everything it sees and regurgitates it. Shows a surprising turn of speed for such a large animal. Serviced by the Jay Bird.

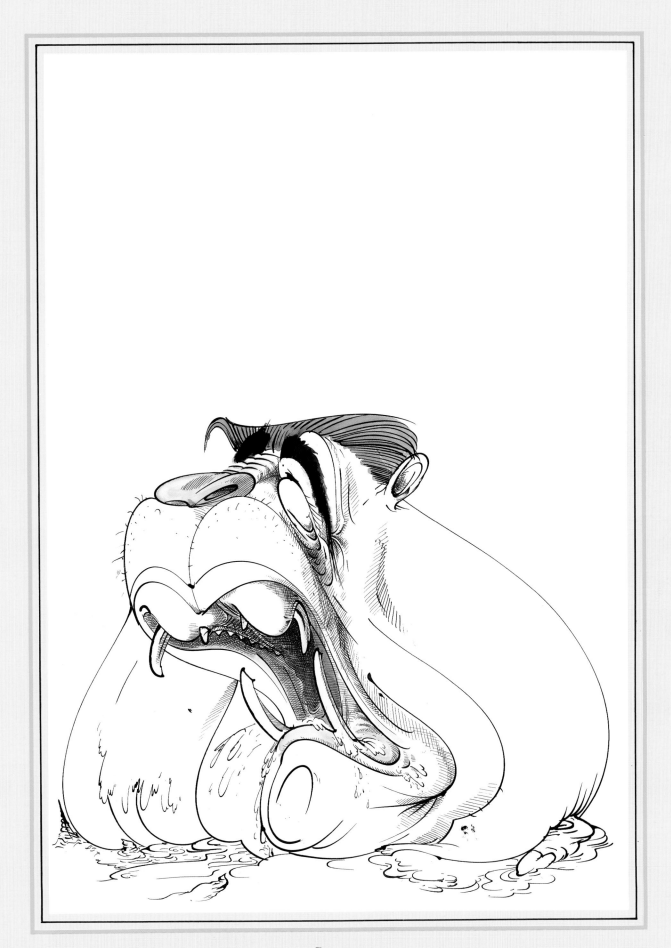

PLATE *39*

§The powerful grey silhouette of the Greedy Baboon appeared walking on all fours along a nearby ridge and lowered himself gingerly onto his favourite rock. He sat deep in thought for some while and then plucked a tiny struggling employee from where he was clinging amongst his soiled and matted fur and, after a few moment's contemplation, popped him into his mouth, chewed and then spat him out. Then he rose and I saw the miracle that thirteen million others saw every morning. The Sun shone out of his bottom. It was astounding. His multicoloured buttocks shone with dazzling headlines: "SOD OFF FOREIGNERS", "A BONK A DAY KEEPS THE DOCTOR AWAY!" "GOTCHA! POOFTER ELTON ATE MY ARGIE" and "THE BIGGEST TITS IN SPACE." The baboon had no shame.

 THE GREEDY BABOON *(Mechanical Digger)*
Habitat: Australia, USA and Great Britain.
Cry: Gotcha!
REMARKS: This Wapping great monster eats trees and regurgitates them as pulp to dull the mind, stupefy and numb brains and addle thoughts. Obsessed with mammary glands. Sky's the limit.

PLATE 40

§Lost in dense foliage Dr Jonathan Stork stood on one leg and looked at it this way. And then he stood on the other and looked at it that way. Strange, it looked the same and yet different both ways. It was all very puzzling.

 Dr Jonathan Stork *(Old Vic)*
Habitat: NW3.
Cry: It depends what you mean by . . .
REMARKS: Tends to fly off in several directions at once.

PLATE *41*

§ *The Gold Fish undulated slowly and effortlessly, letting the lilting, liquid currency carry him ever upwards. It was so easy – everything he swam through turned to gold.*

§ *In the deep, still water dark shadows moved. They looked like weeds, but they were jealous* Piranha Criticus *lying in wait to bite him to pieces.*

 THE REALLY USEFUL WEBBER GOLD FISH *(Lloyds Bankus)*
Habitat: Sitting in the stalls, taking lots of notes.
Cry: Don't cry for me . . .

PLATE *42*

§The Stag Beatle lay face upwards, on a sunny rock in the middle of the stream. He had fallen in the drink and had floated downstream for some time until someone had helped him out at the Ford. He was now drying out on the rock, but the river still rushed by. He was a likeable fellow and, after sketching, I left him drumming on the dry rock with his little legs.

 THE STAG BEATLE *(Ringo Starrus)*
Habitat: Penny Lane.
Cry: What would you say if I sang out of tune?
REMARKS: Nocturnal. Very fond of Bach.

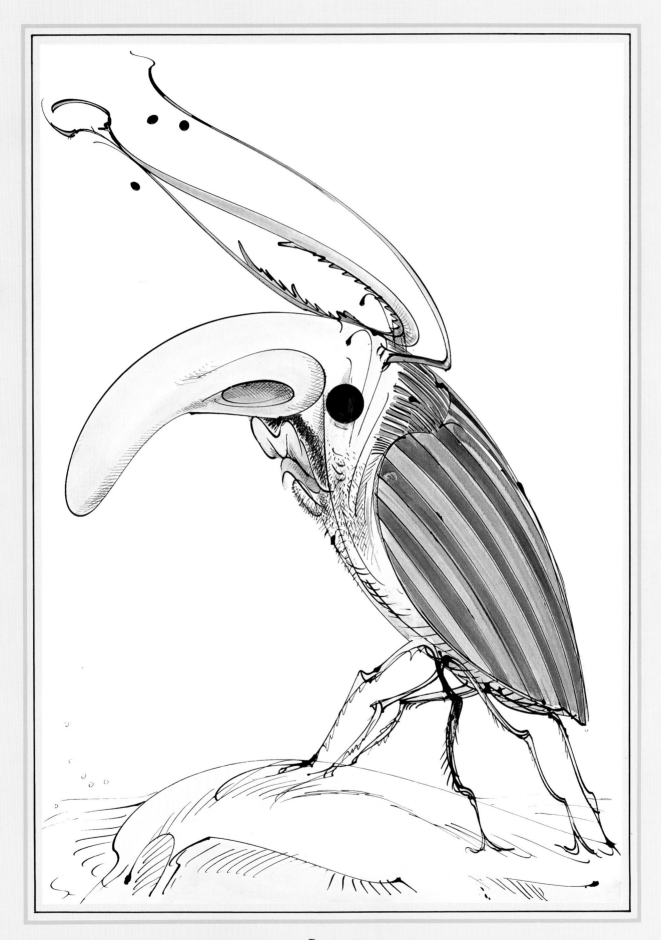

PLATE *43*

§ *After I had finished I fell into an exhausted sleep amongst the remains of my camp. While I slept a reluctant penguin called Christopher took away all my drawings and disappeared into the night.*